Amazing Adventurers

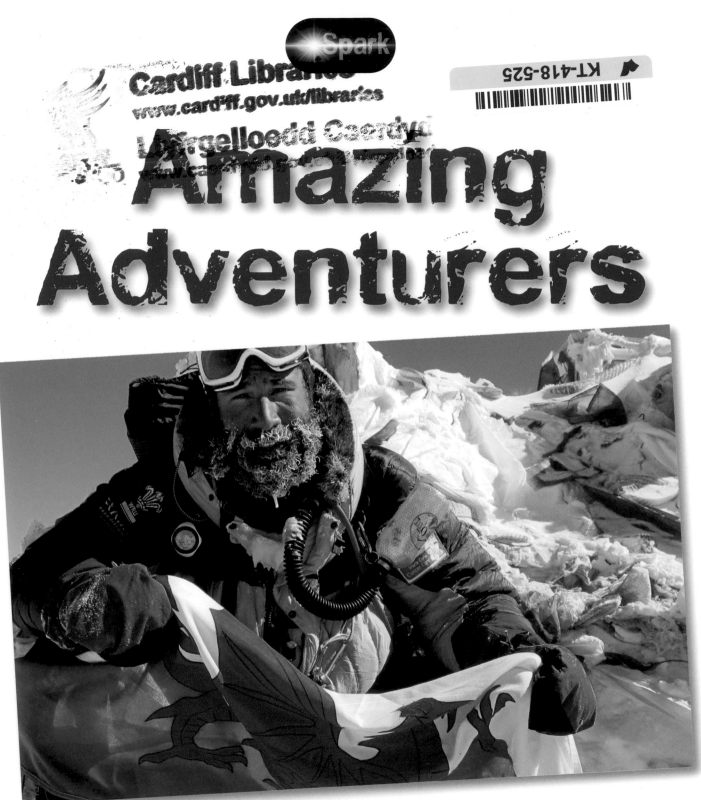

Non ap Emlyn

@ebol

Published by **Atebol Cyfyngedig**, Fagwyr Buildings, Llandre, Aberystwyth, Ceredigion, SY24 5AQ
01970 832 172
www.atebol.com
www.ateducationalbooks.com

ISBN: 978 1 909666 61 0

Project Managers: Dafydd Saunders Jones, Megan Elizabeth Tye
Editor: Gill Matthews
Design: Ceri Jones Studio, stiwdio@ceri-talybont.com
Picture Research: Dafydd Saunders Jones and Megan Elizabeth Tye
Published with the financial support of the Welsh Books Council
Printed by Cambrian Printers, Aberystwyth, Ceredigion

Photographs:
Lowri Morgan Private Collection 3, 4, 16, 17, 18, 19, Getty Images 6, 7, 17, 30,
Maria Leijerstam Private Collection 5, 6, 7, 8, 9, 10, 11, Patagonian Expedition Race 10, 11,
Justin Lotak 11, Solent News and Photo Agency 8, 9, Alamy Images 17, 20, 21
Leo Dickenson 12, 13, 14, 15, Merrell UK, Phil Chappell 4, 5, 20
Richard Parks Private Collection cover, 5, 22, 23, 24, 25
Elin Haf Davies Private Collection 5, 26, 27, 28, 29, 31

Acknowledgements
Atebol wishes to thank Non ap Emlyn for her professionalism during the preparation of these resources.
We also wish to thank all individuals mentioned in this book for their assistance and enthusiasm in being part of this exciting project.

Contents

Living the dream

Wales - a land of adventure

Wales is a land of magnificent mountains, raging rivers and lovely lakes, and is surrounded on three sides by a beautiful coastline and the vast ocean. It's no wonder, therefore, that thousands of people flock to the country each year to have an "adventure".

The range of adventure activities is amazing – climbing, mountain biking, sailing, surfing, kayaking, white water rafting, coasteering – and more.

But did you know that Wales has played an important part in some of the most famous adventures in history? It was to Snowdonia that Sir Edmund Hillary and his team came in the 1950s to train for their expedition to climb Everest in 1953. Before that, in 1910, it was from Cardiff that the ship, the *Terra Nova,* carrying Captain Scott and his team, left for the Antarctic in their attempt to be the first to reach the South Pole.

Today, Wales has a host of modern-day adventurers who set themselves challenging goals in their search for adventure. They are prepared to experience harsh weather conditions, travel across difficult terrain, take part in gruelling activities and endure tough conditions – as you will see ...

Could you be an amazing adventurer? Find out by taking the quiz on page 30.

Maria Leijerstam

So hot! ... So cold! ... So tough! ... So amazing!

Have you ever thought what it would be like to run across an extremely hot, sandy desert? Maria Leijerstam knows exactly what it's like!

Maria was the first Welsh woman to complete the **Marathon des Sables** – a marathon across the Sahara Desert, in Africa – in 2007. This is one of the most difficult foot races in the world!

The Marathon des Sables - 2007:

Day 1:	half marathon
Day 2:	full marathon
Day 3:	full marathon
Day 4:	double marathon ... yes – a double marathon!
Day 5:	rest day
Day 6:	full marathon
Day 7:	half marathon

Profile

Name:	Maria Leijerstam
Born:	Aberdare
Career:	First job: rocket scientist Then: business consultant Now: businesswoman and adventurer
Hobbies:	Travel, sports, adventure

So hot!

How did you feel before the race?
I was scared that I wouldn't be able to do it. I had never run in temperatures of around 48 °C before but I was excited that I was about to run across the Sahara Desert.

What was the weather like?
Hot (48 °C) and very, very dry during the day, but cold at night (5 °C).

How did you cope with the heat?
I wore a cap with a flap on the back to protect my neck from the sun and I wore a sarong, a long piece of cloth, over my head at midday. I drank a lot of water and took salt tablets to replace the salt I was losing through sweating.

What was the most difficult aspect of the race?
The distance wasn't too bad because I got fitter each day and so I began to enjoy it more. The heat was the toughest part for me because I prefer the cold and the snow!

How did you feel as you crossed the finish line?
Exhausted, but very satisfied. I had run the race with two friends of mine and the fact that all three of us finished the race made it extra special.

"The Marathon des Sables was what sparked my desire for more adventures!"

So cold!

In 2012, Maria cycled across Lake Baikal, in Siberia, Russia, and became the first woman to win the Siberian Black Ice Race.

Key data:
- 900 km or 559 miles
- very cold – approx. -40 °C

Maria's diary: memorable moments

Day 1

I was nervous last night – not about the distance but about the cold and the ice. What would I do if I fell through the ice? Would I sink to the bottom?

Setting off was really tough! I had to push the bike because of the deep snow and the ferocious wind.

Day 2

Last night was cold (–27 °C) but I was nice and warm, thanks to all my kit. I could hear a deep thundering noise beneath me – the ice was cracking!

Today was a long day. I cycled for 10 hours, stopping for 5 minutes every hour. I came across black ice – I could see straight through it. I was petrified!

Day 3

Great ice to begin with, with a gentle tail wind and sunshine. Fantastic! I hit a top speed of 47 kph. Then, there was a large field of broken ice and I had to carry and push the bike.

A long day – my knee was painful after cycling for 10 hours yesterday and I fell off my bike twice!

Day 4

I cycled with two other competitors today. After 2 hours, we heard what sounded like thunder and about 20 metres behind us a massive 200 metre long crack appeared. We pedalled hard!

We then saw more 200 metre long cracks in the ice. I decided to check the ice and so stood on my left foot and poked the ice with my right. The ice broke and I sunk thigh deep into the smashed ice and water. Matt grabbed my jacket and pulled me out. So cold!

Day 5

Snow and wind! Couldn't cycle quickly because of my painful knee and I was just not able to stay on the bike!

Day 6

Cycled for 12 hours, stopping every hour for a 5 minute food and drink break. The snow got deeper and deeper and I had to push and pull my bike through it. Quite an effort!

Day 7

The end of the race (Hurrah!) but I couldn't find the finish line! I had to climb through someone's back garden before I could see the finish flags.

Felt delighted and ready to go again. I joked that maybe I should cycle back again!

So tough!

What next – after a hot challenge and a cold challenge? Only one of the hardest adventure races in the world – the Patagonian Expedition Race – in February 2013!

Success for Welsh adventurer

Maria Leijerstam, from Wales, has reached the finish line in the Patagonian Expedition Race, in South America.

Along with three team-mates, she competed against teams from other countries, including Japan and North America, in the 700 km race.

This was no ordinary race as the competitors had to show how they could cope with very difficult terrain and atrocious weather. They also had to take part in a variety of sporting activities:

- **cycling** great distances
- **swimming** across raging rivers
- **trekking** through bogs and dense forests
- **abseiling** down a cliff
- **crossing** a glacier
- **jumping** over deep crevasses
- **kayaking** across a lake, weaving their way through massive icebergs.

"It was unbelievably tough," said Maria. "It was like nothing I have ever done before. One minute I was fighting my way through dense Patagonian forests, the next I was jumping over crevasses and the next kayaking past floating icebergs."

The team slept for only three or four hours each night in order to make good time.

Of the eleven teams, only four managed to reach the finish line, including, of course, Maria's team.

What a truly magnificent performance!

So amazing!

Maria was soon off on another adventure, this time cycling across the Antarctic to the South Pole in December 2013.

A special tricycle was designed for her which meant that she could cycle in a recumbent position – almost lying on her back with her feet positioned out in front of her. The bike therefore remained stable even when the strong Antarctic winds were blowing ferociously.

It was a gruelling journey. It was so cold that even the sweat inside her boots froze! She faced snowstorms that were so extreme that she could not see where she was going and had to rely on her GPS.

Maria was not the only one cycling in Antarctica at this time. Two men on upright bikes were also trying to reach the South Pole. Although they had started three weeks before Maria, she finished before them, becoming the first person ever to cycle to the South Pole from the edge of the continent. Amazing!

"Adventure can be found in many forms and nothing is impossible."

Eric Jones
Life is an adventure

Mountaineering ... skydiving ... paragliding ... base jumping ... Eric Jones has done it all!

Who is he?
- probably Britain's most successful solo climber
- an adventurer – he has been on expeditions to Cerro Torre and Torre Egger on the southern ice cap in Patagonia, Mount Dhaulagiri in Nepal and on two expeditions to Mount Everest
- a well-known skydiver
- a famous base jumper
- a paraglider
- a hot-air balloonist
- a TV and film stuntman.

In 1996, Eric Jones jumped onto the North Pole from a helicopter.

How it all started
When Eric was at primary school a well-known climber, Dr Charles Evans, visited the school accompanied by two sherpas from the Himalayas. He was fascinated by the fact that they had come from a distant country. He, too, wanted a life of adventure.

Profile

Name:	Eric Jones
Born:	1936
Career:	To begin with: Military policeman Then: Factory worker Adventurer who has also featured in many films Now: Café owner
Hobbies:	Cycling, walking, climbing, skydiving, base jumping, skiing, paragliding and riding motorbikes

Eric, the mountaineer

When did you begin climbing?
In 1962.

Where?
One day, a friend and I visited Snowdonia where we saw people climbing the steep rock faces. We were impressed and so we decided to attend a mountain school where we learnt the basics: how to use a rope, how to climb safely etc. After buying some equipment, we started climbing.

What happened then?
After a while, I started solo climbing – climbing by myself – as my friend decided to stop climbing. It was good. I really enjoyed it.

Is this form of climbing dangerous?
Yes, very dangerous. I felt frightened at times, but I learnt how to control my fear. I started on the easier climbs and then went on to the more difficult ones – in Snowdonia, the Dolomites and the Alps.

"You should never try climbing by yourself until you are very experienced, fit and strong. One mistake can be fatal!"

Eric became the first British climber to climb solo on the North Face of the Matterhorn, the Central Pillar of Brouillard and the Bonatti Pillar on the Dru in the Alps.

He was also the first British climber to climb solo up the north face of the Eiger, in the Alps. This is one of the toughest climbs in Europe.

He climbed on Dhaulagiri, in the Himalayas, in 1977 and he filmed the first ascent of Mount Everest without oxygen in 1978.

"Life is adventure or nothing at all."

"Climbing is only one of the joys of being in the mountains. You also have the beauty, the solitude and the feeling of being at one with nature."

During the winter of 1974, Eric began to climb the Matterhorn but the weather was atrocious. He was engulfed by an avalanche; his feet were frostbitten and so he had to postpone the climb and return during the summer months.

Eric, the base jumper

Eric is also well known as a base jumper. In 1986, he abseiled down the side of the Eiger, cleared the ice off a ledge and then ... jumped, with the aid of a parachute! He was the first person ever to do this.

He jumped off a number of buildings and bridges in the USA, but perhaps his most famous jump was off the Angel Falls in Venezuela, South America, aged 61 years old. This is the world's highest waterfall, with a 3,200 foot drop. To train for this jump, Eric did several practice jumps from hot-air balloons.

In 2003, Eric jumped into the Cave of Swallows, Mexico, when he was 66 years old.

Eric, the balloonist

In 1991, Eric and three companions flew a hot-air balloon over Mount Everest.

Danger over Everest

Eric Jones and his fellow-adventurers had a narrow escape recently as they tried to fly their balloon over Mount Everest.

As they were approaching the side of the mountain, one of the burners in the balloon failed and the balloon started drifting towards the mountain. "The mountain seemed to be coming nearer and nearer," said Eric Jones.

It seemed as if the balloon was about to crash into the side of the ever-growing mountain.

To make things even worse, Eric was standing in a barrel strapped to the **outside** of the basket. However, he managed to climb up and solve the problem.

And so, what could have ended in disaster has led to Eric and his fellow-adventurers being the first people to fly over the highest mountain in the world in a hot-air balloon. Congratulations!

Lowri Morgan
The ultra experience

This adventurer has taken part in very gruelling ultramarathons and other exciting adventures.

When she was 18 years old, Lowri had a serious knee operation and was told that she would never run properly again. Since then, she has run in many marathons and ultramarathons.

Profile

Name:	Lowri Morgan
Born:	Gowerton, Swansea, 1974
Hobbies:	Music, singing, playing the viola, extreme sports, skiing, running, scuba diving, swimming
Career:	To begin with: Music teacher Then: TV presenter Now: TV presenter and producer; global adventurer and ultra runner

Diving into the deep

Lowri has dived to the wreck of the Titanic.

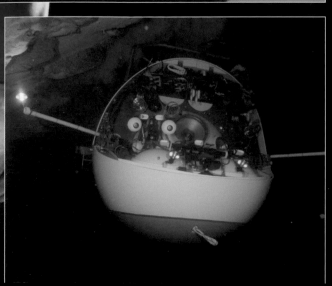

Titanic journal: 2003

Today was incredible. I spent 11 hours in an MIR submersible in the ocean, about 400 miles from Newfoundland, exploring the wreck of the Titanic.

It took us 2.5 hours to get to the bottom and then we spent approximately 6 hours exploring the ship. The first thing I saw at the bottom was a huge rock of coal, which had probably come from the Welsh coal mines. I then saw personal belongings lying on the sea bed, which saddened me. I thought about the travellers, many of them hoping to begin a new life in America. How cruelly their dreams had come to an end!

I felt as if I was on a rollercoaster of emotions during my tour of the ship. On the one hand, I was so excited to see this amazing ship, but it was also a very sad experience.

This has been a once-in-a-lifetime experience. I think that I am one of about 100 people to have ever visited this wreck. What an honour!

The Amazing Jungle Ultramarathon

In 2009, Lowri took part in the Amazon Jungle Ultramarathon – an extremely difficult race, through the dark jungle in very, very hot temperatures.

Facts and figures
- Only 55 of the 120 runners finished the race.
- Lowri was in the top ten.
- She was the 2nd fastest amateur and the 3rd fastest female.
- This was her first ultramarathon.

How did you keep going?
I thought of the tortoise. It is a slow animal, but it perseveres and always gets there in the end. If I was willing to work hard, persevere and be determined enough, I knew that I could do it.

My feet were a mess and I was in pain but my mind took over. It's amazing what the mind can do! When I thought I could no longer carry on, I realised that putting one foot in front of the other meant being one foot closer to the finish line – and then the pain disappeared.

"I kept on plodding – the plodders always get there in the end!"

The 6633 race

In 2011, Lowri took part in another ultramarathon – the 6633 race, an extreme 563 km or 350 mile race held in the cold environment of the Arctic.

Facts and figures
- This race is one of the toughest races on the planet!
- In 2011, Lowri was the only competitor to finish the race.
- So far, only eight people in the world have ever managed to complete this race.

Why did you want to run this race?
This wasn't a competitive race for me but a personal challenge. I wasn't looking to break any records or compete against others. I just wanted to push myself to see how far I could go.

How did you feel during the actual race?
I was happy on the ice road - I had to convince myself that I was. I could not let the mundane but beautiful landscape or the pain I was feeling affect my positive attitude. The fear of failure far outweighed any pain I felt – it kept me going on ... and on ... and on.

"I never gave up because I concentrated on just putting one foot in front of the other."

Ultra running

How did you prepare for your ultramarathons?
I had to train to be strong physically and mentally.

For the 6633, I trained 30 hours a week and ran 150 miles a week. I ran up and down Snowdon. One day, I ran a 46 mile race around the Brecon Beacons and then ran home – a total of 105 miles in 21 hours. I also trained with the Special Forces in Sweden and I ran in huge freezers.

I had to prepare for day-to-day things too – like getting into my sleeping bag and learning how to cook blindfolded because when you're exhausted, after all the running, cooking the dehydrated food can be very difficult.
I therefore had to know how to do it without even thinking about it.

What were the best aspects of these ultramarathons?
I kept reminding myself why I run. I love the space and freedom it gives me and the beautiful countries I race in. The people I have met along the way have inspired me. I also love to push the boundaries and plod on – never giving up.

"They say that there is no glory in practising but if you don't practise there will be no glory!"

Adventure in Namibia

Lowri has experienced other kinds of adventures too.

Namibia journal: 2012

I'm spending a month in Namibia. A TV crew is following my experiences of living with the Himba and the Herero people.

I've fallen in love with the country for its sheer beauty, its wildlife and its people. The scenery changes with the blink of an eye as you drive through it and the landscape is so beautiful.

There aren't many animals here. However, there are elephants that have adapted to live in the desert. We have been camping for most of the trip and sometimes, when we wake up, we see that elephants have passed only a few feet away from our tents!

Another highlight has been flying along Namibia's Skeleton Coast. It has been a genuine 'experience of a lifetime'!

What has made the adventure even more amazing is the kindness and generosity of the people. It is an experience I shall never forget!

"The world is getting smaller and there are so many adventures out there that I would like to pursue – in Wales and further afield. Adventure is in my blood!"

Richard Parks

737 Challenge ...
The Yak Attack ...
and on to the South Pole ...

"Never be scared to follow your dreams. Achieving them isn't always easy but with hard work, self-belief and a smile, anything is possible."

Profile

Born:	Pontypridd, south Wales, 1977
Early career:	Played rugby for Wales. Also played for Pontypridd, Leeds, Perpignan (France) and Newport Gwent Dragons

A new beginning

In May 2009, Richard had to retire from professional rugby due to an injury. Being a very positive person, he decided that he was going to set himself a new challenge. He therefore created the **737 Challenge** – he was going to climb the highest mountain on each of the world's seven continents and stand on all three poles within seven months. What a challenge!

Richard had never set foot on a mountain before deciding to take on this adventure. He therefore had to spend 18 months training and preparing for his challenge.

During the expedition, Richard skied to the North and South Poles, climbed very steep rocks, trekked through dense jungle and deep rivers – and, of course, climbed to the summits of the highest mountains on the world's seven continents. He also faced many difficulties – he collided with his sled at the North Pole, suffered from frostbite on Everest and had a nasty fall on Denali. He had to endure extremes in temperature, from -46 °C at the North Pole to 42 °C in Papua New Guinea.

The expedition was a truly magnificent experience and after 6 months, 11 days, 7 hours and 53 minutes he completed the 737 Challenge on 12 July 2011 – more than a fortnight within his target.

7 Summits
3 Poles
7 Months

"After reaching the summit of Everest safely, my first feeling was just relief. After that it was just gratitude. It really was an incredible moment in my life."

The Yak Attack

In March 2013, Richard took part in the Yak Attack, which is the highest mountain bike race in the world, held in the Himalayas. He cycled a distance of 400 km or 248 miles - up and down steep mountains, across suspension bridges over deep valleys, through streams and mud. He had to experience extreme temperatures – from approximately 30 °C to -15 °C.

"It was tough but it was a privilege to be able to race it and awesome fun (it doesn't always have to be fun to be fun!)."

The Jungle Ultra

In May 2013, Richard set off on another gruelling challenge, The Jungle Ultra race in the Amazon jungle in Peru - this time through dense jungle and deep rivers (some chest high) in extremely hot temperatures (up to 38 °C) and with 100% humidity. He completed the 230 km/142 mile race in 39 hours and 3 minutes over 5 days.

Skiing solo over Antarctica

On 4 January 2014, Richard set a new record for the fastest ever solo unsupported and unassisted journey to the South Pole by a British person. He also became the first ever Welsh person to complete a solo unsupported and unassisted journey to the South Pole.

He skied from Hercules Inlet to the South Pole, a journey of 1,150 km or 715 miles, in 29 days, 19 hours and 24 minutes.

It was a brutal journey with snowstorms, sastrugi (long ridges of snow) and extremely cold temperatures.

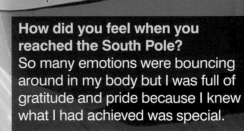

How did you feel when you reached the South Pole?
So many emotions were bouncing around in my body but I was full of gratitude and pride because I knew what I had achieved was special.

Elin Haf Davies
On stormy seas

This adventurer has rowed and sailed across three of the world's oceans.

Elin's adventures began when she was 18 years old, when she left Wales and went to work in an orphanage in Lesotho.

"I think that everyone should have a thirst for adventure and try new things. Each day should have a new experience or adventure as part of it."

Since then, she has had many other adventures and has faced many challenges. She has:
- played rugby for Wales and London Wasps
- cycled from Paris to London
- rowed across the Atlantic Ocean
- run marathons in the Sahara
- rowed across the Indian Ocean
- sailed across the Pacific Ocean
- swum across Bala Lake
- carried the Olympic Torch.

Profile

Name:	Elin Haf Davies
Born:	Parc, near Y Bala, north Wales, 1976
Work:	To begin with: Children's nurse Now: Specialist in children's medicine at the European Medicine Agency
Hobbies:	Extreme adventures

The Atlantic Ocean

On 2 December 2007, Elin and a friend, Herdip Sidhu, set off on a journey across the Atlantic Ocean. 77 days later, she became the first Welsh woman to row across the Atlantic Ocean.

"When I told everyone that I was going to row the Atlantic, they said, 'You'll never do it!'. This made me even more determined. It's so important to do what you really want rather than listen to negative comments!"

How much experience of rowing did you have before you set off?
None at all. I had no idea what I was letting myself in for but this made it even more exciting.

What were the best aspects of the journey?
The sun rising every morning was always the best part. It marked another safe and successful night at sea and the pink, orange and red colours painted the sky beautifully.

What were the worst aspects?
The blisters on my hand and the sores on my bum!

What did you do all day long?
Row! We also slept, ate and daydreamed about having a pizza to eat.

Key data:
Distance: 2,552 nautical miles or 4,726 km
Time: 77 days, 7 hours and 37 minutes

The Indian Ocean

Rowing across the Indian Ocean was a completely different experience. This time, she was a member of a female crew of four. They left Australia on 19 April 2009.

Key data:

Distance:	3,139 nautical miles or 5,813 km
Time:	78 days, 15 hours and 54 minutes

WoodVale
THE WORLD'S TOUGHEST ROWING RACES
www.woodvale-challenge.com
Ocean Rowing

Elin's diary: memorable moments

6 June 2009
Had the best day ever today! The weather was just so beautiful. Blue skies, warm sun and the sea was calm like a pond. So we all went swimming – all four of us at the same time. It was such great fun. The sea was so clear and there were colourful fish everywhere!

1 July 2009
Having a really tough time today. We had to stop rowing as the weather was just too rough. Huge waves kept crashing us off our seats and Sarah got hurt. Being stuck in the cabin listening to the noise of the storm outside is a nightmare. We're all pretty frightened at the moment.

The Pacific Ocean

On 1 April 2012, Elin and a crew of 17 set off on another adventure, this time to sail across the Pacific Ocean. Elin had never sailed before, so the first thing she had to do was learn all the skills she needed.

Key data:
Distance: 5,680 nautical
          miles or 10,519 km
Time: 30 days

What next for Elin?
She'd really love to cross all the Oceans. Having crossed three already, she's now eager to cross the Arctic and Antarctic Oceans.

"In life, you have to decide what you want to do for yourself. Don't just follow the crowd."

Quiz

Have you got what it takes to become an amazing adventurer?

Find out by taking our quiz.

1. Sometimes, adventurers have to spend days, weeks or even months alone as they pursue their adventure. Could you cope?

   a. Yes, of course! This would be quality time with ME. I'd get to know myself better.

   b. I like to be alone sometimes and so I'd be fine – as long as I could send and receive messages.

   c. I'm a social animal – I need people around me all the time (and my dog!).

2. Some adventurers aim to break speed records by racing in difficult conditions. How do you rate your racing ability?

   a. I pace myself carefully but push myself to my limits.

   b. I'm turbocharged to begin with but I tend to slow down towards the end.

   c. I tend to follow the leaders. I don't really like racing.

3. Top adventurers have to face all sorts of difficult situations and sometimes when things are really tough they have to persuade themselves to carry on. How good would you be in really difficult situations?

   a. I'd think beyond the hardship and concentrate on how good it would feel to achieve my goal.

   b. My motto is, "Sometimes you win, sometimes you lose".

   c. I don't think that putting yourself under any strain is good for you.

4. Which one of the following statements best suits your attitude towards adventure?

   a. "Flying solo to the moon (and back)"? Bring it on!

   b. A **little** adventure never hurts anyone.

   c. I'm quite happy as I am, thank you.

Answers

Mostly a: You certainly have a sense of adventure. We can already hear you shouting, "North Pole, here I come!". But make sure you plan and prepare before embarking on any adventure!

Mostly b: You seem to be ready for a life of adventure but just need a little push, perhaps.

Mostly c: You seem to be perfectly happy living your day-to-day existence – and there's nothing wrong with that, but wouldn't you like to have just a **little** bit of excitement in your life?

Glossary

Ascent	an upward climb, e.g. up a mountain
Base jumping	jumping from a fixed object, e.g. a rock or a building, using a parachute. BASE stands for Buildings, Antennas, Spans (bridges) and Earth (cliffs).
Crevasse	a deep crack in thick ice or rock
Expedition	a special journey, e.g. to explore, to carry out research etc.
Foot race	a race run on foot
Glacier	a huge mass of ice that is moving slowly across the land
Global	across the globe
Iceberg	a mass of floating ice
Knot	unit of speed over water equivalent to one nautical mile per hour
Nautical mile	unit of distance over water equivalent to 1,852 metres
Paragliding	jumping from a high point using a special type of parachute and harness to glide to the ground
Sherpa	a person from the mountainous region of Nepal. As sherpas are familiar with the mountains, many of them help mountaineers who go to the region to climb. They act as guides and help to carry the heavy gear.
Skydiving	jumping from an aeroplane and falling freely before opening the parachute
Solo	alone
Stuntman	someone who takes on an actor's role when difficult stunts and dangerous scenes are filmed in television programmes or films
Submersible	a small vessel that can operate underwater
Terrain	landscape
Three poles	the North Pole, the South Pole and Mount Everest
Trek	a long journey, usually on foot
Ultramarathon	a marathon that is longer than the usual 26.2 miles or 42 km
Unassisted	without assistance
Unsupported	without support